This book is dedicated to my children - Mikey, Kobe, and Jojo.

Copyright © 2025 Grow Grit Press LLC. All rights reserved. No part of this book may be reproduced in any form without permission in writing from the publisher. Please send bulk order requests to info@ninjalifehacks.tv

Paperback ISBN: 979-8-89614-112-9
Hardcover ISBN: 979-8-89614-114-3
eBook ISBN: 979-8-89614-113-6

Printed and bound in the USA.
NinjaLifeHacks.tv

Ninja Life Hacks®
by Mary Nhin

Choice Ninja

A Social, Emotional Story About Peer Pressure and Saying N.O.P.E.

Ninja Life Hacks®
by Mary Nhin

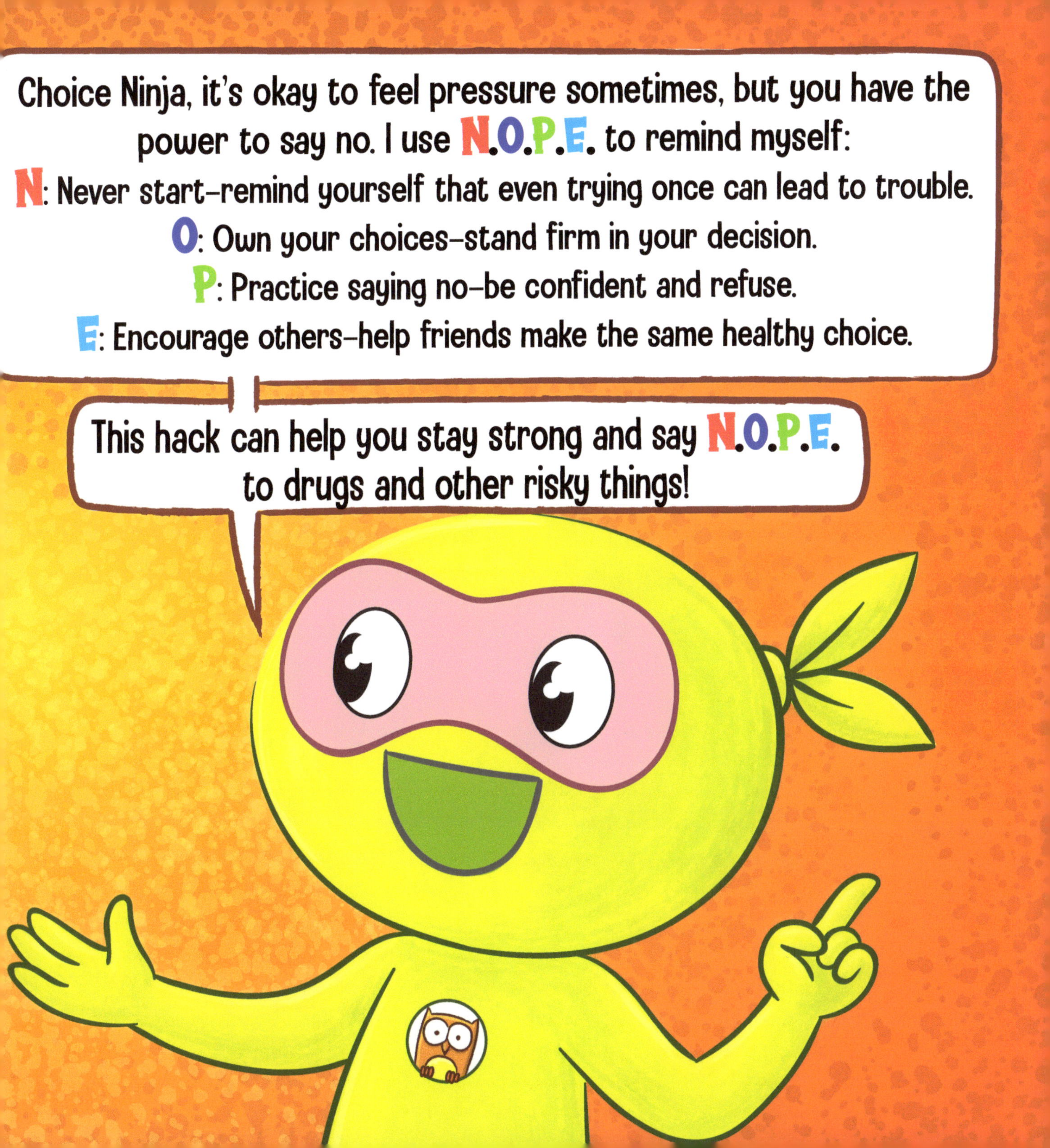

Choice Ninja, it's okay to feel pressure sometimes, but you have the power to say no. I use **N.O.P.E.** to remind myself:

N: Never start—remind yourself that even trying once can lead to trouble.
O: Own your choices—stand firm in your decision.
P: Practice saying no—be confident and refuse.
E: Encourage others—help friends make the same healthy choice.

This hack can help you stay strong and say **N.O.P.E.** to drugs and other risky things!

Remembering the N.O.P.E. strategy could be your secret weapon against peer pressure and help you say no to drugs and other risky things!

Check out the fun Choice Ninja lesson plans at ninjalifehacks.tv

I love to hear from my readers. Email me your feedback or thoughts on what my next story should be at info@ninjalifehacks.tv   Yours truly, Mary

 @marynhin   @officialninjalifehacks   #NinjaLifeHacks

 Mary Nhin   Ninja Life Hacks

 Ninja Life Hacks

 @officialninjalifehacks

www.ingramcontent.com/pod-product-compliance
Lightning Source LLC
LaVergne TN
LVHW070437070526
838199LV00015B/528